...वात्मसमर्पणं पर विर...ली श्रीकृष्णचैतन्यम् सर्वा...

...नाश्रमकारि बहुधा...   ...मकार न...

...स्त्रार्पिता नियमि...   ...गवन्ममार्गा...

...प्तावशी तव कृपा भगवन्ममापि भगवन्ममापि न...

नि दुर्दैवमीहशमिहाजनि नानुराग: तव भगवन्ममाक्षीन...

तृणादपि सुनीचेन तरोरिव सहिष्णुना सहिष्णुना मा...

अमानिना मानदेन कीर्तनीय सदा हरि: सदा आनन...

...म न धनं न जनं न सुन्दरी कामये कीर्तनीय सदा ह...

...ए कवितां वा जगदीश: कामये सदा जन्मनीश्वर आ...

...नो मम जन्मनि जन्मनीश्वरे मा विषमे भवाम्बुधौ

...भवतादकिञ्चनहेतुकी त्वयिविषमे भवाम्बुधौ...वताद्व...

...वि नन्दतनुज! किङ्कर किङ्कर अयि नन्दतनुज!मा...

SMARANAM

{A Garland of Kirtan}

MANDALA
PUBLISHING

Mandala Publishing
17 Paul Drive, San Rafael, Ca 94903
Phone (415) 526-1380 Fax (415) 532-3281
info@mandala.org www.mandala.org

Design by:
INSIGHT DESIGN

Call of visit our website for
a free catalog of books and CDs

SMARANAM
{A Garland of Kirtan}

MANDALA
PUBLISHING

10 9 8 7 6 5 4 3 2
ISBN: 1-886069-49-2
Printed in China through Palace Press International

CONTENTS

INNER ALCHEMY 4

DIVINE LOVE: The Highest Treasure 6

SURRENDER: The Key to the Spiritual Treasure House 12

THE HOLY NAME 18

MOVING WITHIN 24

DIVINE DESCENT 34

CHAITANYA LILA 40

BHAKTISIDDHANTA Saraswati Thakur 42

BHAKTIVINODE THAKUR 48

AGNI DEVA 56

SONGS AND TRANSLATIONS 58

INSTRUMENTS 74

78 .... BIBLIOGRAPHY

79 .... TRACK LIST

80 .... CREDITS

INNER ALCHEMY

MEDITATION MEANS LISTENING to divinity and allowing it to enter our conscious minds and hearts. When we engage in a dialogue with God, an inner alchemy occurs. We become transformed at every level of self. Whether through prayer, song, or action, when we turn our attention to the spiritual reality, we have the ability to change who we are and evolve greater capacities for love within ourselves. When we surrender to God, we become unattached to things of a relative nature and see that what unfolds in our hearts is of utmost concern. In truth, Spirit is calling us to engage in a higher existence of love.

Taking responsibility for ourselves means gaining freedom from our worldly attachments. This is only guaranteed when we are committed to something that is higher than our present concerns. Only when we think of love, which truly has the power to create greater realities for us, can we conceive of the happiness and harmony that our hearts seek.

The inner life of meditation is like a garden in which we can invest our central hopes and desires. Through carefully planting the proper seeds and cultivating them, our hearts will bear the fruits of all that we truly desire. With every prayer and remembrance of the Lord, we contribute to the beautiful reality of this garden, which we may one day fully enter.

The fullness of divinity is experienced in a consciousness beyond matter and time. Love requires a spiritual orientation—a move away from our obsession with the needs of body and mind. Through relationships we are given the context in which we can grow to God consciousness. Thus, to enlighten the world with love, God himself descends and shares with us a glimpse of his divine activities. He also comes to give the world his holy names by which we can connect with his divine reality. By developing an internal relationship with his spiritual pastimes, *lila*, and mantra, or divine name of God, we grow inwardly and can embrace the sacred. By these two keys, we can open the door to our highest potential as spiritual beings.

Sri Chaitanya, the Radha-Krishna avatar who descended in the sixteenth century, admitted us into this process of spiritual alchemy. He is bestowing devotion upon all living beings. By chanting the Holy Names which he taught and recollecting the accounts of his divine activities, we can realize this basic need of the self—true love of God.

Smaranam is a collection of remembrances of Sri Chaitanya through which we can cultivate this divine awareness.

THERE IS A WELL-KNOWN legend about the great sixteenth century Vaishnava saint, Sanatan Goswami. At one time an important government minister, Sanatan took up a life of a renunciation after meeting Sri Chaitanya and became an ascetic in the sacred forest of Vrindavan. There he became illuminated with the light of love of God.

In the meantime, a very poor man named Jivana Chakravarti had gone to Benares where he spent many years worshiping

DIVINE LOVE:
THE HIGHEST TREASURE

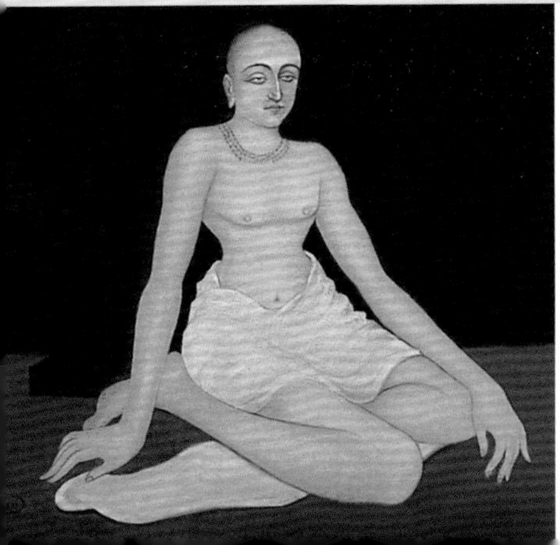

the god Shiva, praying to him for worldly riches. One night in a dream, Lord Shiva mercifully appeared and told him to go to Vrindavan and see Sanatan, who possessed untold wealth he would willingly share.

The poor brahmin immediately set off for Vrindavan where he

found Sanatan rapt in meditation. However, when Jivana saw his thin form dressed in only a dirty loincloth, he began to doubt that Sanatan could give him the riches he was seeking. Even so, he began to tell him of his dream.

On hearing the brahmin speak, Sanatan came back to external consciousness. After listening to him, he replied that he lived humbly, begging only a few crumbs from a number of different houses everyday to maintain his body, and that it would be impossible for him to grant Jivana the kind of wealth he desired.

Jivana Chakravarti was disappointed and turned away, thinking that perhaps Lord Shiva's dream message had been an illusion. At the same time, Sanatan pondered why Shiva had sent the brahmin to him. As he reflected on this, he remembered a philosopher's stone—a mystic stone that grants all one desires—that had long been lying in a nearby garbage pile and was now covered over in dust. As soon as this came to mind, he sent someone to fetch the brahmin and tell him to take the valuable jewel from the rubbish heap. When the brahmin saw the priceless gem, he was overjoyed and thought, "Now I will be the richest person in the entire world!"

After walking some distance away, however, Jivana began to wonder why Sanatan had neglected such a valuable possession. Indeed, if he cared so little for the philosopher's stone, he must own something of even greater value. He began to think that perhaps he had been cheated! What treasure could Sanatan possess that made him care so little for the touchstone?

Jivana quickly ran back to Sanatan and expressed his doubts, asking him if he had anything more valuable in his possession. Then Sanatan told him there was no greater wealth than love of God and that material objects were insignificant and simply a cause of distress. The brahmin then bowed his head and prayed to Sanatan to please give him the wealth that made him consider a magic gem a mere trifle. Sanatan was moved by his prayer and mercifully bestowed upon him the wealth of divine love.

The hidden jewel in the hearts of saints is divine love of God. It is the most coveted treasure of inner life. Like the philosopher's stone, the jewel of divine love transforms everything it touches. By pure devotion to the one Supreme Lord, we attain wisdom and freedom from our struggles within our environment. When we withdraw from all self-centered endeavors and embrace the reality of divine love, we experience a higher world. The soul who seeks nothing other then the service of the Lord receives unconditional love—spiritual love.

To abide in the realm of spirit, we must set aside whatever is highly esteemed in this world and be fully attentive to the ways of the Lord, who is absolutely spontaneous, sweet and playful. The yogi sits in cautioned awareness, but the devotee of God is irresistibly pulled into the ocean of transcendental consciousness by the waves of love. By pure devotion, our hearts are attracted out of the predicament of time and our addiction to the ephemeral is cured.

What characterizes spiritual love? It is that which surcharges the day-to-day world with beauty. Consciousness, the living principle, animates the world of nature and makes it aware of itself. Consciousness is the reality on which divinity plays. Thus, spiritual love signifies the activities of the heart when it is directed by the tides of divine consciousness.

To truly understand this, we must learn the language of love, an inner language based on unconditional surrender and devotion to God. Ultimately, the Lord himself takes us along the spiritual path to the infinite realm where he eternally displays his unlimited mercy and affection.

When our hearts are turned toward the Lord, we find the most comfortable home. In the Lord's eternal drama, we may find a role as a tree, a blade of grass, a stream, or even as a particle of earth. But when we are given such a position, we find that every atom of our existence experiences complete fulfillment. There, even the smallest graces the Lord bestows are felt in all their true magnitude. To be in the presence of the Lord's divine servitors, to even lie in the path worn by their footsteps, is felt to be a most exalted state.

In that world, everything is so

high, so accommodating, so alive and worthy of the highest worship! The most astonishing thing, however, is that when we enter the spiritual world through pure devotion and give ourselves to the Lord, he himself feels immeasurable joy. He feels indebted to us and is captured by our love.

You may have heard of Bilvamangal Thakur's famous devotional work, *Krishna Karnamrita*, an account of the spiritual pastimes of Lord Krishna. A legend is told about the power of the author's deep loving surrender to the Lord.

Bilvamangal was living a depraved life when one day he underwent a change of heart, becoming disgusted by the lust that ruled him. In desperation, he gouged his eyes out so he would no longer be able to look upon the objects of this world with the desire to enjoy them.

His next step was to go on pilgrimage: he set off for Lord Krishna's sacred land of Vrindavan. Being blind, he kept losing his way, but a kind boy appeared to help him. Without this child's assistance, he would have been helpless, so he was happy to accept his aid and carried on with great diligence along the way to Vrindavan.

The child was none other than Krishna himself who had come to accompany his dear servant. The mischievous Lord began to play with his beloved devotee: sometimes he would take Bilvamangal by the hand and show him the way, then suddenly he would run off. Bilvamangal would try to hold onto his hand, but to no avail.

Bilvamangal exhibited the highest degree of tolerance that is characteristic of great devotee saints, but the Lord was absolutely playful, according to the nature of divine love. Every time his guide disappeared, Bilvamangal would experience helplessness and total dependence, but this only served to deepen his devotion.

When Bilvamangal finally deduced that the child who had been with him all this time was Krishna himself, he laughed and said to the Lord, "You may do this as often as you like. You may run off without me, leaving me helpless in my blindness. But I tell you that if you are truly the lord of my heart, you can never leave me."

Those who know the Lord to be their very life's sustenance keep him sealed in their hearts. By the power of their love, they are in the presence of the Lord, wherever they may turn, wherever they may go. Krishna is captured by their love. The legend of Bilvamangal Thakur shows how the Lord takes full charge of those who have surrendered to him. He becomes controlled by their devotion and never abandons them.

TWO FACTORS ARE ALWAYS at play on the path of spiritual development: the unconditional grace of the Lord and our commitment to his service.

We get our ability to dedicate ourselves from the Lord's devotees. Such great saints come into our lives to teach us the holy path of surrender. Their ideal lives are our guiding light; they are the source of faith and spiritual strength; they are the embodiment of the Lord's grace.

SURRENDER:

THE KEY TO THE SPIRITUAL TREASURE HOUSE

We may not have much qualification for spiritual life, but the Lord is always seeking to provide us with the means to attain him. He thus gives us the gift of association with his dear ones. He is merciful, but we must seek the fulfillment of his mercy by following the path of surrender.

The strength of our commitment to the Lord is tested by a difficult journey. As pilgrims, unless we are willing to face the hardships that present themselves, the inner world may never open up. There are common hardships, difficult passes to overcome: attachment to hunger and bodily cravings; the need for stability, understanding, and happiness; and the desire for freedom from the cycle of birth and death. To those who exclusively seek these ends, the all-beautiful face of divinity will remain unknown.

We must see all such obstacles as the direct grace of the Lord, inducing us to surrender. The holy path of devotion requires a strength we can only get from the Lord when we give ourselves with absolute determination. He makes it possible for us to move swiftly over one mountain to another. Our only guide on this journey is our faith, and that too he provides. If we recognize his guidance from within and without, we experience the divine in a personal way at every step.

There is an ancient story about the great sage, Narada, who was traveling to see Lord Narayan in his spiritual abode. On his way he met a brahmin, a member of the Hindu priestly caste. The brahmin was glad to see Narada and asked him where he was traveling that day. Narada answered, "I am going to see our Lord Narayan." The brahmin requested, "If you see our Lord, please ask him when he will be merciful to me and accept me into his company." Narada agreed and moved on his way.

In another province, Narada came upon a cobbler sitting underneath a large hanging banyan tree. Upon seeing the great sage, the cobbler bowed respectfully and greeted him with a warm smile and folded hands. He asked Narada, "Where are you going today?" "I'm going to see our Lord Narayan," Narada replied. After chatting politely the cobbler asked, "Respected one, please ask our Lord when I will have his merciful *darshan*." Narada agreed and left shortly after, making his way into the spiritual realm where he met the Lord.

There he saw Narayan seated on his throne, assisted by many goddesses of fortune. He paid his respects and came before the Lord. After meeting and lovingly exchanging stories, Narada prepared to travel back to the material world in order to continue the work of enlightening others on the path of devotion. Before leaving he asked the Lord, "Lord, I have two questions for you. I met two people today, a cobbler and a brahmin. They want to know when you will allow them to see you. How should I reply to them?"

"For the brahmin, let him know it will be many lives before he will see me. As for the cobbler, inform him that he will come to me very soon," the Lord answered.

Surprised, Narada questioned, "My dear Lord, how is it so that such a qualified and pure brahmin will receive your mercy later, but the cobbler will come upon your special grace so much sooner?"

"Dear Narada, you will soon understand. Just tell them that

their Lord was threading an elephant through the eye of a needle." The Lord then blessed Narada to continue on his way.

Narada descended to the world of time, down to the earthly plane. He came upon the brahmin seated before his temple, reading the scriptures. The air was pleasant with the aroma of sandalwood incense and the brahmin was anointed with beautiful *tilak* and sandalwood. Upon seeing Narada he rose from his seat with folded palms and received the great sage. Eagerly he inquired, "Narada have you seen our Lord?" Narada nodded in confirmation.

"What was he doing?"

"He was threading an elephant through the eye of a needle."

The brahmin hesitated and considered whether or not Narada was teasing him. He dismissed the comment, feeling that perhaps he didn't understand Narada's divine persona. The brahmin asked him whether or not the Lord had responded to his previous question. Narada told him that it would be some time before he would be graced with the Lord's company.

Narada then traveled on further and met with the cobbler. The cobbler was overjoyed to see him again and arose with folded hands to greet him. After kind words and offering him water and a seat, he softly questioned, "Narada, did our Lord mention when I will see him next?" Narada said, "You are greatly blessed. The Lord said that you will receive his company soon."

The cobbler accepted these encouraging words and continued, "What was our Lord doing?" Narada explained, "He was threading an

elephant through an eye of a needle." "How wonderful!" the cobbler replied, reflecting on the mercy of his Lord. Curious, Narada asked him, "What makes you reply in this way? Do you actually believe this could be?" The cobbler replied, "Why not? My merciful Lord can pass hundreds of elephants through the eye of a needle without harming a single one of them." He picked up a small object from the earth and said, "Just see! Within this single banyan seed lies the potential for a huge tree, just like the one I am sitting under. If my Lord has the intelligence and capacity to create something as wonderful as this, why couldn't he do what you have told me as well? For him everything is possible."

Then Narada could understand:

the cobbler's simple faith and humility would allow him to shortly enter the Lord's eternal abode.

Faith is the root from which all true devotion stems. It is the basis of the path of surrender and pure devotion to the Lord. True faith recognizes that by serving the Lord, all other concerns are taken care of. Such faith comes from the grace of saintly people and from hearing the sacred texts. This faith leads us to an acute awareness of the need to fulfill the desires of the Lord and we thus arrive at the gate to the temple of *bhakti*. There we may enter the life of self-surrender—sharanagati.

Surrender to the Lord is a process that grows in devotional life. Without the spirit of selfless dedication, our daily activities are mechanical and lifeless. When we take up the process of surrender, all our actions become spiritualized. They become vehicles that foster wisdom and devotion in us.

In the devotional scriptures it is stated that there are six aspects of surrender. The first two are to accept what is favorable and to reject what is unfavorable to devotion. We should always see that the Lord is maintaining us in all circumstances and to feel that he is our only protector. Then we must be humble and completely self-surrendered, feeling that nothing of true value could be achieved without his grace. When we take up such a life of dedication and apply these six attitudes, we move into the realm of devotion.

THE HOLY NAME descends from the world of divinity to bring us through the passage of time to the awareness of the sole person that creates and sustains all. Chanting the Lord's name is the sacred route that reveals the essence of beauty to the purified heart. It resurrects the consciousness of the soul. It is the single means to attaining pure love of God.

There are paths of selfless work (*karma-yoga*), yoga and meditation (*ashtanga-yoga* or *raja-yoga*), but none of them can lead us to

THE HOLY NAME

this all-auspicious end. The Lord sends forth his holy name and the spiritual guide to draw us back to our home in the eternal realm.

There is an episode in the life of Hari Das Thakur that highlights the transformational power of divine sound. Hari Das Thakur is considered the great preceptor in the chanting of the holy names of God.

When Hari Das was still a young man, he moved to a secluded part of the Benapole jungle in West Bengal where he performed spiritual practices throughout the day and night. All the people in the area observed his spotless character and staunch devotion to the Holy Name and respected him for it.

At that time, there was a powerful landowner in the area named Ramachandra Khan. He became envious of Hari Das Thakur's increasing reputation and plotted to ruin him by uncovering some character flaw. Hari Das was a great saint and so all of the attempts the landowner made were of no avail. Finally, Ramachandra called some prostitutes together and asked them to seduce him. One of these prostitutes, a very beautiful young girl named Lakshahira, promised to accomplish the task within three days. Ramachandra gleefully engaged her in his conspiracy. Ramachandra wished to expose Hari Das immediately after his fall. He proposed sending an armed guard with Lakshahira to take the ascetic prisoner as soon as he had been defiled. Lakshahira refused, however, saying that it would be better to wait until she was sure her efforts to seduce Hari Das had been successful.

That night she dressed up in her most seductive attire and went to Hari

Das's hut. Attempting to appear as a pious Hindu lady, she first prostrated herself before the holy tulasi plant he worshiped. She then went and stood beside Hari Das, brandishing all the charms at her command. Flirtingly, she mouthed, "You are a very handsome man, Thakur. You are in the full bloom of youth. What woman would be able to resist you? I have come here because I am filled with desire for you. If I don't get your touch, I will kill myself."

Unflinchingly he answered, "I have just begun chanting my regular number of Holy Names. As soon as I am finished I will do as you wish. While waiting, please sit down and listen to the sound of the Holy Name." He kept chanting and chanting until morning. The prostitute became impatient and left; she returned to Ramachandra Khan and told him the whole story.

That night she came again to Hari Das's hut. He expressed his regret at failing to fulfill her desires due to his inability to complete his quota of Holy Names. Once again, however, he assured her that as soon as he was finished, he would do whatever she wished. As before, Lakshahira bowed to the tulasi plant and sat down. She spent the night waiting for Hari Das to finish his chanting.

When morning came, she again grew restless. Hari Das said to her, "I have taken a vow to recite the holy name of God 10,000,000 times before the end of the month. I am almost at the completion of this vow. As a matter of fact, it should be finished this very night. As soon as it is over, I can sleep with you. Do not worry."

On the third night Lakshahira returned, again bowing to the tulasi plant and sitting down beside Hari Das to listen to him chant. As she continued to listen to him chanting, the contaminants in her mind began to melt away and she began to regret her mission. Finally she fell down at his feet and begged his forgiveness. She told him about Ramachandra Khan's evil intentions.

Hari Das answered her, "I know all about Ramachandra Khan's wicked plans. I would have left on the very first day but I wanted to show you my mercy, so I stayed for three days."

Lakshahira then asked him to instruct her so that she might be saved. Hari Das asked that she donate any money she had saved to the brahmin priests. Furthermore, he said, she should come and take up residence in his hut where she should chant the Holy Names constantly and worship the sacred tulasi plant.

Lakshahira did exactly as Hari Das instructed her, donating all her wealth to the brahmins, shaving her head and dressing in a simple cloth before returning to the hut. She then started to recite the holy mantra of the names of God three hundred thousand times daily as Hari Das did. By virtue of worshipping the holy tulasi plant and chanting the Holy Name, she became very renounced. Freed from the passions of the mind and heart, she attained pure love of God. Through Hari Das Thakur's mercy, the prostitute became a great saint and many came to receive her blessings thereafter.

The holy name of the Lord frees the mind from deliberation on the temporal and concentrates the intellect on the divine. Once withdrawn from the distractions of the sensory world, the intellect becomes illuminated by the Holy Name. It empowers us to distinguish relative from absolute necessities in our lives and gives us the power of forbearance, allowing us to remain steady in our search for true love.

Saints have captured the highest beauty in their hearts—for them the Holy Name becomes a boundless, overflowing vision of the Lord. They are no longer stricken by the limitations set by time on the consciousness of conditioned souls, for they have reconciled the dualism of the sensory world and their attention is drawn instead into the world of harmony. Through this vision of unity they take part in the higher existence of divine love.

We must receive the holy mantras, the transcendental names of God, from great devotees, for they have seen the spiritual nature of the Name. The saintly devotee, like a doctor, sows the seed of divine love in our heart, which releases us from the dream of mundane life. When we receive the mantra from a self-realized soul, the sound conception they impart is a living connection to our inner realities.

To find such a friend, a true friend of the soul, amounts to achieving the highest fortune. The selfless devotee is like a great current that directs us back from our wayward course into the ocean of love. He draws mind and heart to that place of consciousness where the lord of love resides.

Simply repeating the names of God will not quickly settle the mind and purify the heart. But when we invoke the Lord of the Name, striving to please and serve him—such chanting burns away the passions of the mind and ignites the soul with the inner cognizance of spirit. With a sincere heart, one should recollect the meaning of the Holy Name and attract the Lord by his or her soulful prayer. Then comes a new beginning—the Holy Name draws us into a wholly separate affair from our present world of experience. The self, exalted in divine ecstasy, receives an incessant desire to serve the lord of the heart.

If the name of God is sung with firm conviction, the heart will soon be cleared of all ignorance and the true knowledge of the eternal relationship between the soul and Krishna, the lord of love, will be established. By unceasing meditation on the Divine Name we grow fully conscious that it is non-different from the personality of God.

TODAY, AS WE STEP into a new millennium, we are coming to grips with our universal need to understand our inner life—to develop ourselves internally, contemplatively, to integrate deeper spiritual values into our everyday lives. We find meditation circles, prayer groups, and online spirituality chat rooms springing up everywhere. There seems to be a general movement toward a deeper awareness of the spiritual.

The information age encourages a rapid exchange of ideas. Within

MOVING WITHIN

this phenomenon is the rebirth of values from our common past. Scholars of religion are unearthing more and more information about our spiritual heritage, giving us the opportunity to be more thoughtful in our approach to spirituality. At the same time, novel insights from the fields of psychology and the social sciences are fueling a greater understanding of our human evolution. These developments indicate that the rapid changes of the modern world need to be met with a sanity that comes from within. We need to move with solid spiritual footing as we grow outwardly in the technological world.

Further, we need to develop a richer language for our inner life so all our outer "advancement" will be tempered by a necessary stability. Isn't this what we aim for with all our knowledge—the wisdom to see everything in its proper place? The internal must open up so the external will have meaning and value. With such intuitive vision everything in our life will find its harmonious position.

Much has been done to demystify spiritual experience. The works of Freud, Jung, Maslow and Wilber have taken us from an awareness of the personal to the spiritual domains of our being. Modern scholarship and communications, in turn, have made it possible for us to learn from the masters of the East, ancient and modern, like Padmasambhava, Dogen, Shankar and Aurobindo. With this research has come an expanded awareness of our inner landscape, of humanity's common spiritual heritage.

More and more people it seems are having spiritual or "peak" experiences. Greater opportunities to come in contact with bona fide spiritual teachings and teachers definitely benefit our spiritual growth. But, can we say that we've come to a final plateau in our understanding of spiritual truth? Many seem to believe in or experience God or higher states of consciousness, but few know about the esoteric and deeply personal devotional realms of experience.

Truth is infinite and thus so is revelation. To attain enlightenment—satori, a peak experience, a non-dual state, whatever you wish to name it—is not the end of conscious experience. We should not forget that spiritual love is a reality, that potential for such love is within every one of us. Consciousness has quality, activity, and involves reciprocation with the divine. We are consciousness. *Aham brahmasmi* says the Vedic idiom. Therefore, the foundation of our spirituality must be a search for the deeper truths of transcendence, honoring the soul by exploring our personal relationship with God. We must voyage within to seek out the hidden treasure of devotion. When we come to the end of that journey, the mystery of divinity comes alive and reminds us of the true joys of life. That is when we will relish *smaranam*, moments spent in remembrance of the Lord.

Taking as provisions the accumulated spiritual values and knowledge we have received through the vast communication that is afforded in our times, we should begin our journey inward. Knowledge of the great philosophies and theories of different mystical traditions and the life histories of great saints is inspiring, but only a life of practice bears real fruit. Everyone must take his own journey. Knowledge alone cannot substitute for the raw and unmediated experience of the Spirit, for that alone truly transforms the self.

The lamp of the pilgrim is the

mantra. It is of the fabric of the spiritual sky—self-luminous. The mantra of the holy names of God is given by the spiritual guide to help us unlock the doors of spiritual perception. When we truly experience the nature of the holy names of God, the wisdom of the scriptures and the sages become our reality.

All struggles faced on this journey to God have a transforming power on the consciousness of the individual. Through the process of loving surrender, the light of spirit begins to radiate through the coverings of the limited self. Purifying the habits of the mind, the heart is left freer and more loving. And when we have penetrated the once-dim material consciousness, a heavy rush of spirit rolls in to reveal the unearthly beauty of the Lord's divine form. Having arrived in the inner sanctum of our souls, we there find the personal Being that underlies all existence. The Vedic scriptures declare this to be the highest achievement (*param-artha*) in human existence.

The Biblical tradition tells us that man is made "in the image of God" and that man's ultimate destiny is to achieve his likeness to God. This is a symbolic expression of our capability to transform internally—spiritually. Our limited perception of the sense world can evolve into a recognition of God's all-pervading personality. At the end of the spiritual journey, the soul becomes an eternal soul mate of the Lord, capable of experiencing a relation of personal intimacy with Him. This objective is at the heart of all religions. When we attain this stage, *smaranam* becomes our natural state of being.

Love means to be tied by the bonds of constant remembrance.

We have compared the mantra to a guiding light on the journey to union with the Beloved. Song and prayer are vehicles that facilitate this vital inward voyage. As reminders of the Beloved's divine beauty, they quicken our step and bring joy to what can sometimes be a long and wearisome travail.

To effectuate the kind of inner transformation that bears the fruit of spiritual love, it is not enough to simply sit down for meditation, prayer, taking a half-hour appointment with our breath, or watching our passing thoughts. It requires full dedication. All our day's activities must be seamed together by remembrance of our goal. Taking up contemplative life means connecting all of our senses and activities in the remembrance of the Lord. Our mind may not be concentrated and clear, but it can be easily transformed when we perform our daily work as a service to the Lord. Then the dichotomies of life, material and spiritual, self and other, become integrated in the light of devotion. The life of contemplation is a celebration of our unique chance to grow with every waking moment.

The key to wedding our spiritual ideals and daily activities is found in the cultivation of a personal God-centered spiritual practice that is guided by kirtan, spiritual song. Sacred song liberates our vision. Those whose hearts have been captivated by the divine can find divinity in even the turning of a leaf. Such people are the everyday mystics—everything reminds them of the Lord and they remain absorbed in God consciousness through the Lord's holy names. Their minds are naturally drawn to the Lord who is all-attractive, but this same transformation takes place in us when we come to see the Lord everywhere and at all times through the power of the Divine Name.

Through kirtan, the relative and absolute become harmonious. In the contemplative life, we engage all our works in the service of the Lord, chanting the Holy Name with dedication and faith. This is the alchemy of inner transformation. By accompanying our every activity with the divine sound, anything that takes us away from divine consciousness becomes distasteful and the heart gradually begins to perceive divinity in the sounds of nature, in others and within ourselves.

Our lives should thus be seen as an organic whole, to be offered in devotion to the Lord. Prayer, meditation, song, dance, writing, cooking, art and dialogue—all are jewels in the contemplative life, providing us with opportunities to enter into a dialogue with God. Though these activities have potency to awaken a deeper realization of God, kirtan takes pride of place as the most powerful of all. Through the Holy Name, perception of the Lord's holy form arises in the purified heart. He is free to reveal himself at his own will. Our finite consciousness cannot fit him within our limited conceptions. We cannot reach God, the fully spiritual, by mere mental and intellectual exercises, yet he does become perceivable through divine sound.

So, in our walk toward the destination of love of God, meditation on the names of God (*kirtan)* is the most effective tool at our disposal. Remembrance (*smaranam*) cannot be achieved directly; it comes quickly, however, as the byproduct of proper attentiveness to the Name. Through such attentiveness, we experience the fully transcendental nature of the Holy Name, which then delivers waves of divine love into our hearts.

Of course, as with any journey, the pilgrimage on the path of devotion centered on kirtan has its signposts that tell us where we are and how to proceed. The course of spiritual development begins with hearing. Listening to divine discourses and receiving the mantra purify the mind and plant a spiritual conception in our heart. Thus, hearing spiritual sound vibrations is sometimes compared to sowing the seeds by which the thousand-petaled lotus of consciousness will bloom. We realize the inner meaning of the mantra by watering the heart with constant chanting.

In contemplative life, connecting activities to the divine is called *abhyasa-yoga*. This prepares the mind for deeper reflection, *manana*. We reflect on discourses we have heard, on the mantras we chant, and by recognizing the feelings we experience while doing so. Serious reflection then awakens *smarana*, divine remembrance of the Lord. This is how we move from the external to the internal life.

Swami B.P. Puri advises us in his modern classic, *Art of Sadhana*: "One engaged in external devotional practices should still make added efforts to meditate on the Lord, for external practices are meant to remind one of the Lord and from there lead to reflection, which once achieved, allows for one's easy engagement in constant meditation."

Raghava Chaitanya Das further outlines the stages of development of God consciousness in his work, *The Divine Name*. We have discussed in brief the stages leading up to remembrance of the Lord: receiving the mantras and hearing spiritual discourses (*sravana dasha*), accepting those teachings (*varana dasha*) which is followed by the stage of practice (*sadhana dasha* or *smaranam dasha*). In this stage of turning within and deepening our meditation, *smaranam* (remembrance), one recalls the Holy Name and qualities of the Lord. *Smaranam* has as its chief aim purification of the heart, but is inferior to the practice of kirtan in its ability to awaken love of God. Here we are discussing the broad stage of internalization before spiritual perfection ensues. Within this stage of the path there are generally five levels of attainment discussed. They are:

Smarana (remembrance)—Recalling in one's mind the holy name, form and qualities of the Lord. This occurs only in flashes in this immature state of meditation.

Dharana (contemplation)—The mind vacillates between the warring senses and wanders from one sense object to another. It is the famous "monkey mind" that is always grasping for something novel. The objective, while one is in this state, is to fix the mind on the Lord through continuous meditation on his names.

Dhyana (constant meditation)—A more intense concentration of the mind on the Holy Name. One has overcome the baser pullings of the mind and senses and gathered himself within, experiencing an "inner posturing"—the self begins to find freedom and becomes absorbed in the spiritual sound vibration.

Druvanusmriti (concentration)—The incessant flow of the mind on its object of concentration. It is compared to the unbroken flow of oil when poured.

Samadhi (trance)—The spontaneous manifestation of the Lord in the heart. This stage of samadhi is different from the one attained by jnanis (gnostics) generally known by the name *asamprajnata samadhi* (as in Patanjali's *Yoga-sutra*). Bhaktas, devotees of the Lord, attain an uninterrupted realization of the transcendental play (*lila*) of the Supreme Lord through their meditations. Their hearts are the "playing ground of the sweet absolute."

Divine revelation and remembrance is an outcome of proper meditation on the mantras and names of God. Further, we find the awakening of the spiritual identity of the soul and its relationship with the Lord. As one's devotion becomes exceedingly more exclusive and imbued with a divine loving attachment, he or she attains the highest perfection of joining the Supreme Lord in his transcendental lila. This all comes through proper performance of kirtan.

In contrast with most mystical practices, kirtan can be performed even more effectively in congregation. This is the highest and most effective devotional practice for awakening love of God. To reveal this process Sri Chaitanya, the avatar of divine love, propagated the congregational chanting of the names of Krishna in the sixteenth century.

BEAUTY IS THE LANGUAGE of the heart; we all perceive it in our own way. When God descends, the source of beauty is close at hand. What once was remote appears in our world to give us a glimpse of the grand design beyond.

The word "avatar" refers to a divine descent; The entrance of the transcendental reality into the relativity of human history and creation. The divinity makes his appearance in this world to invoke consciousness of him, attracting the minds and hearts of all. In his

DIVINE DESCENT

earthly manifestation he shows absolute independence from any worldly conditions, such as time, space and mortality. This widely accepted phenomenon of the Vedic tradition is his highest act of grace and love. The Vedic understanding recognizes a Godhead who is not distant, but directly related to our personal affairs and predicaments.

The appearance of the Lord within the everyday world is uncommon. Sri Chaitanya, who appeared in the sixteenth century, is considered the last descent of divinity according to the Vedic scriptures. It is written that Sri Chaitanya descended from the realm of transcendence, and made his rendezvous with the commonplace. Although untouched by the laws of nature, he reciprocated with the masses on a human level to teach the process of chanting the Holy Names and to widely bestow divine love of Lord Krishna.

Sri Chaitanya revealed a spirituality that addresses our rational, moral, and practical needs. Yet he emphasized the transcendent emotions of the soul. To Sri Chaitanya, the soul and its ability to share in a divine and eternal relationship with God is the basis of all spiritual concerns. His teaching added a new vision of depth to our spiritual conceptions: a path to valid experience of the higher realms of divine love. His teachings were not bodiless metaphysics or soulless ritualism. They were drawn from the Vedic canon as compiled by the legendary Vyasa Muni. Vyasa is credited with writing down the Vedas, Vedanta Sutras, Bhagavad Gita, Srimad Bhagavatam, Upanishads, Mahabharata and Ramayana. Sri Chaitanya revealed the most esoteric understanding of all these scriptures. Although only the eight verses of the *Shikshastaka* are directly attributed to him, his teachings were recorded and expanded upon by his followers and direct students.

Swami B.R. Sridhar expresses the philosophical and scriptural basis of Sri

Chaitanya's teachings in his *Golden Volcano of Divine Love*:

"Sri Chaitanya Mahaprabhu preached the full-fledged theistic conception given in Srimad Bhagavatam. Srimad Bhagavatam mainly deals with the comparative study of theism and the ontology of Krishna consciousness. It surpasses all other Vedic literatures, even the Puranas. The *Brahma Vaivarta Purana* and *Padma Purana* represent the importance of devotion to Krishna through narration and history to some extent, but fall short of the philosophical and ontological standard set by the 'great Purana,' Srimad Bhagavatam. Srimad Bhagavatam can satisfy all Vedantic scholars, for it represents Krishna consciousness in its fullest dignity. Srimad Bhagavatam expounds as the highest attainment of theism—not consciousness, intelligence, or ontology, but ecstasy, beauty, and harmony—*rasa.* In Srimad Bhagavatam, *rasa* is all-important. It is a unique treatise, for it takes theism from the plane of intellectual jugglery to the domain of *rasa.*"

Rasa is the experience of spiritual beauty that is felt in a divine loving relationship between the soul and God. This transcendent experience was an inner reality that Sri Chaitanya wanted all to aspire to. In the realm of spiritual existence there are unlimited *rasas*, or divine devotional sentiments. Sri Chaitanya revealed that Krishna, the lord of love, was the source of all these unlimited spiritual currents of exchange. He wished to awaken the world to these dimensions of spirituality through initiating the chanting of God's names.

When the Lord descends he does not come alone. He brings forth an entourage of personal associates to engage in loving pastimes, *lila*. Among Sri Chaitanya's closest companions was Sri Nityananda. There is a description of Sri Chaitanya's life in *Chaitanya Bhagavata* that describes their inner identities:

"Previously, Lord Krishna descended with Balaram [said to have occurred approximately 5,000 years ago] and their divine activities and the narration of their divine deeds brought joy to the ears and minds of all living beings. Now these same two divine personages have descended to bring the most coveted treasures of the eternal life to the most common."

Sri Nityananda and Sri Chaitanya gave the matchless gift of love of Krishna. Performing *sankirtan*, congregational chanting of the holy names of Krishna, and propagating this *yuga dharma*, they bestowed their unlimited mercy.

If Sri Chaitanya is the avatar of divine love and the most magnanimous avatar, then Nityananda was the servant of his mercy and made all heirs to that love. Nityananda evoked spiritual consciousness in the hearts of all living beings. It is said that by the mercy of Nityananda, the pastimes of Sri Chaitanya will manifest in one's heart. He is a storehouse of the love of Sri Chaitanya and is widely extending that wealth. He is taking from the ocean of love and bathing all in a current of infinite grace.

Everywhere that Sri Chaitanya went, all the living beings that heard his chanting were immersed in God consciousness. In his recorded life history, the *Chaitanya Charitamrita*, there is a passage that records his journey through the Jharikhanda forest. It says that all the birds, beasts, and plants inhabiting the forest began to chant and dance in divine exultation as he passed through, singing the holy names of the Lord. This is the effect of divine song and was the merciful benediction of Sri Chaitanya upon everyone he met. Swami Sridhar explains:

"This is the all-conquering conclusion. The highest conception of the Ultimate Reality must also be the highest form of *ananda*, ecstasy. Sri Chaitanya Mahaprabhu is Krishna, ecstasy himself, tasting his own sweetness and dancing in ecstatic joy. His own holy name is the cause of his ecstasy, expressed as dancing, and the Holy Name is the effect of his ecstasy, expressed as chanting. The cause is the effect. The dynamo is creating ecstatic energy, which makes him dance, and his chanting distributes that ecstasy to others.

"Because Sri Chaitanya Mahaprabhu comes from the highest position, he cannot give ordinary things. He must give the most valuable thing, and his attention must be drawn to the most needy. Is it unnatural? The highest magnanimity must take notice of the lowest and most needy. And if he wants to help them, he will do so with his own coin. He cannot distribute only glass or stone chips to them. When he has the opulence of jewels, and gems, why should he search for stone chips to distribute to the lowest level? He must extend to the lowest and poorest people what he thinks to be real wealth."

The highest wealth of divine ecstasy—that which makes contemplatives contemplate—was widely distributed in the pastimes of Sri Chaitanya. By remembering the spiritual activities of Sri Chaitanya and performing our devotional practices in line with his teachings, we are transported to the realm of love divine. In the life and precepts of Sri Chaitanya we receive the highest revelation of the teachings of the foremost Vedic scripture, Srimad Bhagavatam. As Srimad Bhagavatam details the inner life of God, Krishna *lila*, Sri Chaitanya's life teaches the highest goals of the devotee of the Lord. In spiritual terms as well as material, the giver is understood to be superior to that which is given. Perhaps Sri Chaitanya's life activities are the most sublime spiritual reality of all. Swami Sridhar illuminates this consideration:

"What is Krishna *lila*? It is the real essence of nectar. It is the gist of sweetness, happiness, and ecstasy. The sweetness of the sweetest thing that can ever be conceived is represented in Krishna *lila*. Then what is Chaitanya *lila*? Chaitanya *lila* is like the fountain from which the sweet nectar of Krishna *lila* flows in hundreds of streams in all ten directions."

FROM BEYOND THE VEIL of mundane experience, Divinity comes to speak to us of eternity. Nearly five hundred years ago this world was inundated with the eternal rhythms of the mystery and power of *sankirtan*. The divine sound of *sankirtan* is a reminder of the wondrous reality; it calls us back out of time and into the realm of transcendental consciousness. The only currency required to receive that wealth is faith, for it is the Lord's merciful promise to attract us to the richness and fullness of spiritual love.

CHAITANYA LILA

Smaranam, a collection of devotional songs in praise of Sri Chaitanya and his associates, is an invaluable compilation for the life of any spiritual practitioner. Agni Deva has performed kirtan in public for decades, bringing pleasure to both the devotional community and music lovers in general. It is the quality of the devotee to

always desire the benefit of others. We are greatly inspired by his latest gift, by which he once again shares the vital message of Sri Chaitanya.

Sri Chaitanya's biographer, Krishna Das Kaviraj, implores us:

"O devotees, come! Come and swim with the swans in the reservoir of Chaitanya Mahaprabhu's pastimes. Krishna *lila* is flowing to the world in countless rivulets from that lake. Like clouds, the devotees draw up nectar from that lake and then pour it down on the fortunate souls, distributing it freely. Come and live in that lake. May the swan of your mind swim in the nectarean lake of Sri Chaitanya Mahaprabhu's life and precepts, from where so many hundreds of streams of nectar are flowing in all directions. O devotees, I offer this humble prayer to you."

May all those who come in contact with these special recordings be touched to take up the process of kirtan and to study the life and precepts of Sri Chaitanya.

PRABHUPADA BHAKTISIDDHANTA Saraswati Thakur holds a unique position in the line of pure devotion to Sri Krishna. In *Sri Prabhupada-padma-stavaka*, the first track of this collection, one of his leading students, Swami B.R. Sridhar, describes him as the embodiment of *Hari kirtan* (divine song in glorification of Lord Hari) and the universal shelter of all those surrendered to Sri Chaitanya. As divinity manifests itself as the Holy Name, it also manifests in the form of the preceptor of the Name. In

PRABHUPADA BHAKTISIDDHANTA SARASWATI THAKUR

Bhaktisiddhanta Saraswati's life and teachings, we see how he bore the current of pure devotion as introduced by Sri Chaitanya and carried into the modern era by his father, Bhaktivinode Thakur.

Bhaktisiddhanta Saraswati appeared as an effulgent, golden-skinned child in the home of Bhaktivinode Thakur in Puri on February 6, 1874. The house was constantly reverberating with the sound of the names of God. Bhaktivinode named his child Bimala Prasad after the feminine aspect of the divinity (Bimala is the divine energy of Lord Jagannath), who allows humanity to enter into the Lord's inner mysteries. The name by which he was later known, Bhaktisiddhanta Saraswati or Saraswati Thakur, was taken by him when he started his preaching mission in 1918.

Bhaktivinode taught his seven-year-old son the rules for worshiping a deity and initiated him into the chanting of the Holy Name. From his youth, Bimala Prasad was trained in all the aspects of devotional practice. He also learned about printing and writing for his future calling in producing spiritual literature.

Bimala Prasad showed a natural talent for mathematics and astrology and in high school spent more time studying astrology and spiritual scriptures than the general curriculum. In 1892, he was admitted to the Calcutta Sanskrit College. There, once again, instead of confining his studies to the college courses, he started systematically reading all the books in the library.

In 1897, Srila Bhaktivinode Thakur established his place of spiritual practice and worship at Svananda Sukhada Kunj, across the river from Mayapur where Sri Chaitanya appeared in this world. It was there, in 1898, that Bimala Prasad first saw his future guru, Srila Gaura Kishor

Das Babaji Maharaj. He was attracted by the extraordinary character of this fully liberated being, who was indifferent to all social conventions, and was initiated by him in January, 1900.

In October of 1898, Bimala Prasad set off on a pilgrimage with Srila Bhaktivinode Thakur. During this time, he began to show the spirit of renunciation that ran throughout his life. While staying in Mayapur in 1905, Saraswati Thakur began publicly speaking the message of Sri Chaitanya and, following in the footsteps of Hari Das Thakur, undertook a vow of chanting a billion holy names of God, requiring a minimum of 300,000 names every day. This demanded more than twelve hours of meditation a day and lasted for almost ten years.

In 1911, Bhaktivinode Thakur sent Saraswati Thakur in his place to Baligha to debate the ritualistic priests, called Smarta Brahmins. They viewed birth as the absolute measure of spiritual status—an argument motivated by their desire to preserve their inherited social power and certainly not based on true spiritual principles. Many branches of Hinduism in the nineteenth century had sought to reform the caste system, and Saraswati

Thakur took this opportunity to formulate his social philosophy, based on the fundamental spiritual equality of all human beings.

Saraswati Thakur argued that devotion to the Lord, recognized in an individual of any social class, is the highest social qualification. Individuals should be measured in relationship to their spiritual development. The primary purpose of the Hindu caste system was to establish a social framework in which humanity would be spiritually uplifted through work and duty, in a harmonious combination of sacred and secular. Saraswati Thakur felt that this spiritual purpose had been lost in time as the upper castes tried to conserve their social privileges.

It was for this very reason that Bimala Prasad accepted the renounced order of life, *tridandi sannyas*, on March 7, 1918, on the occasion of Sri Chaitanya's appearance day. He was known from that day forward as Tridandi Swami Srila Bhaktisiddhanta Saraswati Thakur. This visionary act at once established a respectful distance from the earlier Vaishnava tradition of renunciation, the eremetic life of the six Goswamis, and created a monastic teaching brotherhood to actively spread the teachings of Sri Chaitanya Mahaprabhu. Saraswati Thakur's sannyas was not meant for abandoning the world and society, but for transforming it into a spiritual world harmonized in the service and love of Krishna.

On the day he took sannyas, Saraswati Thakur also established the Gaudiya Math, a spiritual institution whose mission he described as having these imperatives:

"Every selfless welfare worker in the Gaudiya Math should be prepared to expend 200 gallons of his own blood to nourish the spiritual body of every person in this human society... The motto of Gaudiya Math is *param vijayate sri-krishna-sankirtanam*—may the congregational chanting of the glories of Krishna be ever victorious."

In 1921, Saraswati Thakur revived the annual *parikrama* (pilgrimage) of Nabadwip Dham, the holy land where Sri Chaitanya exhibited his pastimes of love. It was also his wish to establish 108 shrines throughout India as memorials to the places Sri Chaitanya had visited. On October 9, 1925, Saraswati Thakur and countless devotees undertook the pilgrimage tour of Vraja-mandala, the holy land of Sri Krishna, stopping at every place where Krishna had engaged in his pastimes almost 5,000 years before.

Saraswati Thakur decided that it was now time to preach Mahaprabhu's message in Europe. He sent three of his senior students to spread the teachings of Bhaktivinode Thakur and Sri Chaitanya in England. Later, in the 1960s, his celebrated disciple A.C. Bhaktivedanta Swami Prabhupada established an international society that took the teachings of Krishna consciousness around the world.

In October of 1921, Saraswati Thakur spent more than a month in Radha Kund keeping vows for the month of Karttik (*niyama-seva)*. During this time, he spoke daily on the *Upanishads, Chaitanya Charitamrita, Srimad Bhaga-*

vatam, and circumambulated the sacred lake, teaching the higher practice of meditation on the eternal cycle of pastimes of the Divine Couple.

At about 5:30 A.M., on Thursday, January 1, 1937, Saraswati Thakur entered the eternal abode, joining Radha and Krishna in their predawn pastimes. Through his life effort, Saraswati Thakur conveyed the ideals of practice and preaching, showing that the stream that passed through Bhaktivinode Thakur will continue to gather force and flow into the world. To this day, we see that many societies of pure devotion have grown out of the root institution of the Gaudiya Math to spread the teachings of the Holy Name and devotion to Krishna.

THE MAJORITY OF THE SONGS found in this collection were composed by the eminent poet-saint Bhaktivinode Thakur. Bhaktivinode was one of the greatest revitalizers of the Vedic tradition, the basis of Indian sacred and secular thought. He revered the concept of universal and divine love over all other goals in life and dedicated his existence to sharing his vision with humanity. He had dreams of a world community that would support the spiritual evolution of each of its members.

BHAKTIVINODE THAKUR

In addition to the large corpus of literary works he produced, the example of his personal life is a beacon of light for others on the spiritual quest. In his later years, Bhaktivinode lived as a solitary mystic. Earlier in his life, however, he was very much involved in Bengal's intellectual and social network. His modern upbringing gave him a practical awareness that aided him in expressing his more esoteric insights and realizations into our spiritual nature.

Bhaktivinode Thakur was born on September 2, 1838, in an aristocratic family of Birnagar, West Bengal, as Kedarnath Datta. From childhood, he excelled in all fields of learning and displayed an extraordinary inquisitiveness for truth. Kedarnath learned the details of the Indian historical epics, Mahabharata and Ramayana, by the age of six and soon after began studying Sanskrit and English. He composed his first poem at the age of eight.

During his period of education, Kedarnath Datta delved into several faiths and wisdom traditions: from Tantra and the various sects of the Hindu tradition to Islam and other practices current in contemporary society. Disenchanted by the hypocrisy he found in many of the traditions' followers and his own inability to find answers to his deeper existential concerns, he moved on to the thought of the West. He scoured the Western philosophical canon, studying the works of Hume, Goethe, Kant, Schopenhauer and others. He also examined the Bible, Koran, and the Brahmo religion.

During his years at Calcutta University in the 1850s, he was well received by the intelligentsia and his English poems were published in the

Library Gazette. He was involved with several forums that met to debate and discuss the literary work of influential Bengali and European writers. Besides proving his talents as a writer, Kedarnath also became a skilled orator.

Kedarnath took up a number of teaching and government posts from the 1860s to 1880s. In these years he went through some major ideological transformations.

As Deputy Magistrate of Dinajpur, he met a local resident, Kamal Lochan Raya, who impressed upon him the teachings of the enigmatic incarnation of divine love, Sri Chaitanya, which had become obscure at the time. When Kedarnath happened upon rare copies of the *Bhagavata Purana* and *Chaitanya Charitamrita*, he eagerly reviewed them, reflecting deeply on their inner meaning. He was so moved by the nature and depth of the answers he immediately found in these two scriptures that he embarked upon a comprehensive study of them.

In that same year of 1868, Kedarnath delivered a historic speech in response to a conflict between the Brahmo Samaj, a neo-Hindu reform movement in India, and the conservative Hindu population, entitled "The Bhagavata: its Philosophy, Its Ethics and Its Theology." In this discourse he voiced his discoveries of the universal spiritual truths that were hidden within the *Bhagavata Purana*, a text that both groups accepted as being from their own spiritual heritage. A glimpse of the liberal spirit that pervaded his search for truth can be seen in an excerpt from this lecture:

"The student is to read the facts with a view to create, and not with the object of fruitless retention. Students, like satellites, should reflect whatever light they receive from authors and not imprison the facts and thoughts just as magistrates imprison convicts in the jail! Thought is progressive. The author's thought must have progress in the reader in the shape of correction and development."

In 1870, Kedarnath Datta accepted the influential posts of Deputy Collector and Deputy Magistrate in Puri, the site of the famous Jagannath temple. It was in this holy city that the legendary Sri Chaitanya Mahaprabhu spent the last twenty-four years of his life on this earth. Kedarnath was very eager to further cultivate his understanding of Chaitanya's teachings and activities. He became deeply inspired by Chaitanya's universal conceptions of spirituality and underwent a deeper study of the theory of devotion as taught by his direct followers.

Kedarnath remained in Puri for five years and scrutinized all of the major scriptures of the Chaitanya tradition and their commentaries. He established an assembly of scholars inside the grounds of the Jagannath temple and publicly spoke on the devotional texts he was studying. Many educated spiritualists came to hear his profound insights on the *Bhagavata*.

At this time Kedarnath Datta became absolutely dedicated to the teachings of Sri Chaitanya. Feeling that the dignity of the Vedic tradition had lost its standing in public opinion, he set out to reform and reinstate it in its pure form. Just as Gautama Buddha radically rejected the socio-religious practices of the Brahminical religion on the pretext that the priestly class was forsaking its societal role for political influence, Kedarnath Datta denied the absolute social status of the Brahmin, as he saw the same signs of misunderstanding in his own times. Like the Buddha, he recognized that the spiritual purity of an individual outweighs his status at birth. Both emphasized the universal potential of all beings to evolve spiritually in this very life.

In 1885, Kedarnath Datta was given the title Bhaktivinode by his guru. One of his contemporaries was so impressed by his extensive groundwork in revealing Chaitanya's teachings that he dubbed him the "seventh Goswami" after Sri Chaitanya's six principal associates, the six Goswamis of Vrindavan.

Bhaktivinode vigorously set out to touch every echelon of his contemporary society with the teachings of Sri Chaitanya. He wrote numerous short stories, articles, poems, songs and spiritual novels. Although externally he was a family man and government administrator, he still managed to produce over a hundred books in seven different languages. His life is the perfect example of what contributions a fully dedicated spiritualist can make to society, culture and religion.

At the turn of the last century, Bhaktivinode began to take a more reclusive attitude toward life. He retired from government service to Puri, emulating the mood of his lord, Sri Chaitanya. Bhaktivinode Thakur moved into an even deeper contemplative life by which he could reflect on the more esoteric and subtle dimensions of devotion. He continued to meet smaller groups of devotees to discuss his insights.

He expressed his deep conviction that the intimate worship of Godhead, employing the path of divine sound to awaken transcendental emotion, is the most exalted form of spirituality. In the spirit of Sri Rupa Goswami, he characterized this position in a famous song: "The relishing of poetic sentiments is not the sacred rapture of devotional poetry. Real sacred rapture is found in the sentiments revealed by the purifier of the age, Gaura. Give up the study of all other subjects and worship the moon of Godruma's forest bowers (Sri Chaitanya)."

In 1914, Bhaktivinode Thakur left this world in Calcutta. His legacy can be found in his untiring devotion to spreading the doctrines of Sri Chaitanya. His literary accomplishments were to make the teachings of devotion accessible to the layman as well as to the learned spiritualist, for although he wrote several complex Sanskrit texts and commented on others, he also translated and wrote books in easily accessible Bengali.

Bhaktivinode was deeply concerned about our spiritual destinies. Sensitive to the needs of the future world community with all the complexities of modern life, he wrote in a clear and simple voice. He laid out a complete system of spirituality, based on divine loving relationship between the self and divinity, which he considered to be the most universal spiritual

truth. His shared realizations give access to the deep unity and subtle aspects of the wisdom traditions.

Bhaktivinode saw the need for a fundamental restructuring of the philosophical vision that has come to be known as "postmodern liberalism." He wished to inspire the thoughtful members of our global community to seek true spiritual satisfaction, to find fulfillment of the deepest needs of the heart. His message was that ritualistic religion, devoid of the true spirit of renunciation, wisdom and knowledge of spiritual emotion, was superfluous to the primary work that we as individuals need to undergo. Bhaktivinode Thakur envisioned a universal spirituality that would shelter everyone under the banner of divine song. His invaluable service of composing devotional songs, which are lucid accounts of his sacred meditations on the divine, will continue to draw us into the higher world of spirit.

Agni Deva was born in Trinidad, West Indies, and moved to New York in his youth. His study of Vedic philosophy led him to discover the devotional music of West Bengal. In 1972 he began publicly performing bhajan and kirtan in the traditional Bengali style. He later toured with the South Asian Cultural Exhibition, singing on university campuses throughout the United States. In his numerous trips to India he has sought out master *kirtaniyas*

A G N I   D E V A

who have helped him evolve a truly traditional style. His influences include the work of A.C. Bhaktivedanta Swami Prabhupada from whom he received mantra initiation into the path of pure devotion following Sri Chaitanya. Along with his musical and spiritual pursuits, Agni

Deva's other passion is cooking. He owns and operates Govinda's Vegetarian Buffet in Santa Rosa, California.

Smaranam is the fifth recording from Agni Deva, along with *Bhakti Rasa*, *Tribute to Prabhupada*, *Treasure of the Holy Name* and *Live in New Dwarka.*

A.C. Bhaktivedanta Swami Prabhupada

Śrī-Prabhupāda-padma-stavaka

HYMN TO SRILA PRABHUPADA'S LOTUS FEET

(Swami B.R. Sridhar)

-1-

sujanārbuda-rādhita-pāda-yugaṁ
yuga-dharma-dhurandhara-pātra-varam
varadābhaya-dāyaka-pūjya-padaṁ
praṇamāmi sadā prabhupāda-padam

His lotus feet are served in devotion by tens of thousands of highly virtuous souls; he is the establisher of the religion of the age (as *śrī-kṛṣṇa-saṅkīrtana*) and the presiding monarch of the Viśva-Vaiṣṇava-rāja sabhā-the universal society of the pure devotees that are the true "kings" or guides of all; he fulfills the most cherished desires

SONGS & TRANSLATIONS

and dispels the fear of all souls. I constantly make my obeisance unto the radiance emanating from the toenails of the holy feet of my Lord, Srila Prabhupada, worshipable by one and all.

-2-

bhajanorjjita-sajjana-saṅgha-patiṁ
patitādhika-kāruṇikaika-gatim
gati-vañcita-vañcakācintya-padaṁ
praṇamāmi sadā prabhupāda-padam

He is the leader of the fortunate souls blessed with the treasure of internal pure devotion; he is greatly merciful to the fallen souls, being their only shelter; and his holy feet are inconceivable to the deceivers who are thus deprived of spiritual beatitude. I constantly pay obeisance to the radiance emanating from the toenails of the holy feet of my Lord, Srila Prabhupada.

–3–

atikomala-kāñcana-dīrgha-tanuṁ
tanu-nindita-hema-mṛṇāla-madam
madanārbuda-vandita-candra-padaṁ
praṇamāmi sadā prabhupāda-padam

I make my obeisance unto his divine, charming yet commanding lofty form of golden hue. That beautiful figure shames the mad ecstasy of golden lotus stems. Venerated by tens of millions of Cupids, the moons of the toenails of my worshipful Divine Master reveal the beauty of his lotus feet. I constantly make my obeisance unto that effulgence emanating from the toenails of the lotus feet of my Lord, Srila Prabhupada.

–4–

nija-sevaka-tāraka-rañji-vidhuṁ
vidhutāhita-huṅkṛta-siṁha-varam
varaṇāgata-bāliśa-śanda-padaṁ
praṇamāmi sadā prabhupāda-padam

Like the moon that delights the stars, he delights the circle of personal servitors who surround him; the sound of his thunderous lion's roar sets to flight all inauspiciousness; while the simple, inoffensive souls attain the ultimate peace by accepting his lotus feet. I constantly make my obeisance unto the effulgence emanating from the toenails of the lotus feet of my Lord, Srila Prabhupada.

–5–

vipulīkṛta-vaibhava-gaura-bhuvaṁ
bhuvaneṣu vikīrtita-gaura-dayam
dayanīya-gaṇārpita-gaura-padaṁ
praṇamāmi sadā prabhupāda-padam

He has expanded the glorious abundance of the land of Gaura's birth; he has broadcast the tidings of Sri Gauranga's supreme magnanimity throughout the whole universe; and in the hearts of the fit recipients of his grace, he has bestowed the gift of Sri Gaura's lotus feet. I constantly make my obeisance unto the effulgence emanating from the toenails of the lotus feet of my Lord, Srila Prabhupada.

–6–

cira-gaura-janāśraya-viśva-guruṁ
guru-gaura-kaiśoraka-dāsya-param
paramādṛta-bhaktivinoda-padaṁ
praṇamāmi sadā prabhupāda-padam

He is the long awaited shelter and Universal Guru for the souls surrendered unto Sri Gauranga; he is absorbed in the service of his Gurudeva, Sri Gaura Kishor Das Babaji; he wholeheartedly adores Srila Bhaktivinode Thakur. I perpetually make my obeisance unto the effulgence emanating from the toenails of the lotus feet of my Lord, Srila Prabhupada.

–7–

raghu-rūpa-sanātana-kīrti-dharaṁ
dharaṇī-tala-kīrtita-jīva-kavim
kavirāja-narottama-sakhya-padaṁ
praṇamāmi sadā prabhupāda-padam

He is the illustrious personality to raise the flag that sings the glory of Sri Rupa, Sri Sanatan, and Sri Raghunath Das; he sings the glories of the powerful personality of brilliant erudition, Sri Jiva, throughout the world; and he has won the renown of being one with the hearts of Srila Krishna Das Kaviraj Goswami and Narottam Das Thakur. I perpetually make my obeisance unto the effulgence emanating from the toenails of the lotus feet of my Lord, Srila Prabhupada.

–8–

kṛpayā hari-kīrtana-mūrti-dharaṁ
dharaṇī-bhara-hāraka-gaura-janam
janakādhīśa-vatsala-snigdha-padaṁ
praṇamāmi sadā prabhupāda-padam

Bestowing his grace upon all souls, he is Hari kirtan incarnate. As the associate of Sri Gaura, he relieves Mother Earth of the burden of offences committed upon her. And he is so gracious that his loving warmth to all beings exceeds even that of a father. I perpetually make my obeisance unto the effulgence emanating from the toenails of the lotus feet of my Lord, Srila Prabhupada.

–9–

śaraṇāgata-kiṅkara-kalpa-taruṁ
taru-dhik-kṛta-dhīra-vadānya-varam
varadendra-gaṇārcita-divya-padaṁ
praṇamāmi sadā prabhupāda-padam

He is a wish-fulfilling tree for his surrendered servitors, fulfilling their heart's aspiration; even a tree is shamed by his magnanimity and forbearance; and even the gods who confer boons on all also worship his lotus feet. I perpetually make my obeisance unto the effulgence emanating from the toenails of the lotus feet of my Lord, Srila Prabhupada.

–10–

parahaṁsa-varaṁ paramārtha-patiṁ
patitoddharaṇe kṛta-veśa-yatim
yati-rāja-gaṇaiḥ pariṣevya-padaṁ
praṇamāmi sadā prabhupāda-padam

He is the crown jewel of the paramahamsas, prince of the supreme perfection of life, Sri Krishna *prema*; he accepted the robes of a mendicant sannyasi just to deliver the fallen souls; and he is attended by the topmost tridandi sannyasis. I perpetually make my obeisance unto the effulgence emanating from the toenails of the lotus feet of my Lord, Srila Prabhupada.

–11–

vṛṣabhānu-sutā-dayitānucaraṁ
caraṇāśrita-reṇu-dharas tam aham
mahad-adbhuta-pāvana-śakti-padaṁ
praṇamāmi sadā prabhupāda-padam

He is the dearest intimate follower of the divine daughter of Vrishabhanu, and I know myself as the most fortunate by taking the dust of his holy feet upon my head. I make my obeisance unto his invincible, wondrously purifying lotus feet; I perpetually make my obeisance unto the effulgence emanating from the toenails of the lotus feet of my Lord, Srila Prabhupada.

Śaraṇāgati

TAKING SHELTER

(Bhaktivinode Thakur)

śrī kṛṣṇa caitanya prabhu jīve dayā kari
sva-parṣada svīya dhāma saha avatari
atyanta durlabha prema karibāre dāna
śikhāya śaraṇāgati bhakatera prāṇa dain-
ya, ātma-nivedana, goptṛtve varaṇa
avaśya rakṣibe kṛṣṇa viśvāsa pālana
bhakti-anukūla mātra kāryera svīkāra
bhakti-pratikūla-bhāva varjanāṅgīkāra
ṣaḍ-aṅga śaraṇāgati haibe jāṅhāra
tāṅhāra prārthanā śune śrī-nanda-kumāra
rūpa sanātana pade dante tṛṇa kari bhaka-
tivinoda paṛe dui pada dhari kāṅdiyā
kāṅdiyā bale āmi ta adhama śikhāye
śaraṇāgati karahe uttama

Out of compassion for the fallen souls, Sri Krishna Chaitanya appeared in this world with all of his eternal associates and his eternal abode.

Wishing to bestow on them that most rare gift of love for himself, he taught *sharanagati*, the process of taking shelter of the Lord that is the life of the devotees.

Humility, self-surrender, accepting Krishna as your protector, the belief that Krishna will save you in all circumstances, undertaking only activities conducive to developing love for Krishna and rejecting everything which is detrimental to that end—these are the six elements of taking shelter, *sharanagati.*

The son of Nanda, Krishna, listens to the prayers of anyone who takes shelter of him in this six-fold process of surrender.

I fall down at the feet of Rupa and Sanatan with straw in my teeth and take hold of them in all humility. Crying, I call out, saying, "I am most fallen. Please teach me how to take shelter of Krishna so that I can perfect my human life."

Śrī Gaura Nityānander Dayā

THE MERCY OF GAURA-NITYANANDA

(Lochan Das Thakur)

–1–

parama karuṇā, pahuṅ dui jana,
nitāi gauracandra
saba avatāra sāra-śiromaṇi
kevala-ānanda-kanda

These two lords, Nitai and Gaurachandra, are most compassionate. Of all the incarnations of Godhead, they are the most perfect, for they are the unique source of joy.

–2–

bhaja bhaja bhāi caitanya nitāi
sudṛḍha viśvāsa kari
viṣaya chāṛiyā se rase majiyā
mukha bala hari hari

Pray, O brothers! Pray with great faith to Chaitanya and Nitai. Give up the objects of sense gratification, absorb yourself in the flavors of their divine mood, and use your tongue to sing the names of Hari!

–3–

dekho ore bhāi tribhuvane nāi
emono dayāla dātā
paśu pākhī jhure pāṣāṇa vidare
śuni jāṅra guṇa-gāthā

Just look, O my brothers! There are no more compassionate benefactors than Gaura-Nitai anywhere in the three worlds. Even the birds and beasts' hearts melt when they hear their virtues.

–4–

saṁsāre majiyā rahili paṛiyā
se pade nahila āśa
āpana karama bhuñjāye śamana
kahaye locana-dāsa

I have fallen into worldly life, completely absorbed in mundane pursuits, and have never aspired to attaining their service. The god of judgment is making me suffer the consequences of my acts, so says Lochan Das.

Dainyātmikā

A HUMBLE PRAYER

(Bhaktivinode Thakur)

–1–

emona durmati, saṁsāra bhitare,
poṛiyā āchinu āmi
taba nija-jana, kono mahājane,
pāṭhāiyā dile tumi

O Lord! I was such an evil person and had fallen into the deepest depths of material life. Then you were so kind that you sent me one of your intimate associates, a great authority on spiritual life.

–2–

dayā kori' more, patita dekhiyā
kohilo āmāre giyā
ohe dīna-jana, śuno bhālo kathā
ullasita habe hiyā

This great person saw how fallen I was and took compassion on me. He said: "O unfortunate one! Listen to me, I have some good news that will make your heart joyful."

–3–

tomāre tarite, śrī kṛṣṇa-caitanya
nabadvīpe avatār
tomā heno kata, dīna hīna jane,
korilena bhava-pār

In order to deliver you, Sri Krishna Chaitanya has descended to the city of Nabadwip. He has helped so many unfortunate and fallen people like yourself cross over the ocean of material life.

–4–

vedera pratijñā, rakhibāra tare,
rukma-varṇa vipra-suta
mahāprabhura nāme, nadiyā mātāya
saṅge bhāi avadhūta

In order to fulfill the Vedic prophecy, he has appeared in a Brahmin family with a golden skin color. Named Mahaprabhu, he enlivens the entire town of Nabadwip in the company of his older brother, Nityananda Avadhuta.

–5–

nanda suta jini, caitanya gosāñi
nija-nāma kori' dāna
tarilo jagat, tumi-o jāiyā
loho nija-paritrāṇa

He who is the son of Nanda Maharaj has now appeared as Chaitanya Gosai, making a gift of his own holy name. By so doing, he has delivered the universe. Now you too should go to him and assure your own salvation.

–6–

se kathā śuniyā, āsiyāchi, nātha!
tomāra caraṇa-tale
bhakativinoda, kāṅdiyā kāṅdiyā
āpana-kāhinī bale

Upon hearing this message, I came here to take shelter of your lotus feet, O Master! Crying profusely, I am telling you the story of my life.

Śrī Śacīnandana Vandana

A HYMN TO THE SON OF SACHI

(Swami B.R. Sridhar)

–1–

jaya śacinandana sura-muni-vandana
bhava-bhaya-khaṇḍana jayo he

All glories to the son of Sachi, glorified by the gods and sages, who destroys the fear of death and rebirth. All glories to him!

–2–

jay hari-kīrtana nartana vartana
kali-mala-kartana jayo he

All glories to the singing of his holy name, to his singing and dancing, to him who cuts through the evil age! All glories to him!

–3–

nayana-purandara viśvarūpa sneha-dhara
viśvambhara viśvera kalyāṇa

The lord of our eyes, the object of his brother Visvarupa's affection, known as Visvambhara, who brings all auspiciousness to the world.

–4–

jaya lakṣmī-viṣṇupriyā viśvambhara-priya-
hiyā jaya priya kiṅkara īśāna

All glories to Lakshmi and Vishnupriya, who are so dear to Visvambhara's heart. All glories to his servant Ishan!

–5–

śrī sītā-advaita-rāya mālinī śrīvāsa jaya
jaya candraśekhara ācārya

All glories to Sita and Advaita, to Malini and Srivasa. All glories to Chandrasekhara Acharya!

–6–

jaya nityānanda rāya gadādhara jaya jaya
jaya haridāsa nāmācarya

All glories to Nityananda Prabhu and all glories to Gadadhar Pandit. All glories to the acharya of the Holy Name, Hari Das.

–7–

murāri mukunda jaya
premanidhi mahāśaya
jaya jata prabhu pariṣada

All glories to Murari and Mukunda, to the gentle Premanidhi. Glories to all the Lord's entourage!

–8–

vandi sabākāra pāya adhamere kṛpā hoy
bhakta saparṣada-prabhupāda

I bow down to the feet of all these associates of the Lord and to the devotee companions of Srila Prabhupada in the hope that they will be compassionate to me.

Kabe Habe Bolo

WHEN, O WHEN, WILL THAT DAY BE MINE?

(Bhaktivinode Thakur)

–1–

kabe ha'be bolo se-dina āmār
(āmār) aparādha ghuci, śuddha nāme ruci,
kṛpā-bale habe hṛdoye sañcār

When, O when, will that day be mine? When will you give me your blessings, erase all my offences and give my heart a taste for chanting the Holy Name in purity?

–2–

tṛṇādhika hīna, kabe nije māni',
sahiṣṇutā-guṇa hṛdoyete āni'
sakale mānada, āpani amāni,
hoye āswādibo nāma-rasa-sār

When will I taste the essence of the Holy Name, feeling myself to be lower than the grass, my heart filled with tolerance? When will I give respect to all others and be free from the desire for respect from them?

–3–

dhana jana āra, kobitā-sundarī,
bolibo nā cāhi deha-sukha-kārī
janme-janme dāo, ohe gaurahārī!
ahaitukī bhakti caraṇe tomār

When will I cry out that I have no longer any desire for wealth and followers, poetry and beautiful women, all of which are meant just for bodily pleasure? O Gaura Hari! Give me causeless devotional service to your lotus feet, birth after birth.

–4–

(kobe) korite śrī-kṛṣṇa- nāma uccāraṇa,
pulakita deho gadgada bacana
baibarṇya-bepathū ha'be sanghaṭana,
nirantara netre ba'be aśru-dhār

When will my body be covered with goose bumps and my voice broken with emotion as I pronounce Krishna's name? When will my body change color and my eyes flow with endless tears as I chant?

-5-

kobe nabadwīpe, suradhunī-taṭe,
gaura-nityānanda boli' niṣkapaṭe
nāciyā gāiyā, berāibo chuṭe,
bāṭulera prāya chāṛiyā bicār

When will I give up all thought of the world and society to run like a madman along the banks of the Ganges in Nabadwip, singing and dancing and sincerely calling out the names of Gaura and Nityananda?

-6-

kobe nityānanda, more kori' doyā,
chāṛāibe mora viṣayera māyā
diyā more nija-caraṇera chāyā,
nāmera hāṭete dibe adhikār

When will Nityananda Prabhu be merciful to me and deliver me from the enchantment of the sense objects? When will he give me the shade of his lotus feet and the right to enter the marketplace of the Holy Name?

-7-

kinibo, luṭibo, hari-nāma-rasa,
nāma-rase māti' hoibo vivaśa
rasera rasika- caraṇa paraśa
koriyā mojibo rase anibār

When will I buy, borrow or steal the ecstasies of the Holy Name? When will I lose myself in the intoxication of the Holy Name? When will I immerse myself in the nectar of the Holy Name after grasping the feet of a saint who constantly relishes the flavors of devotion?

-8-

kabe jībe doyā, hoibe udoya,
nija-sukha bhuli' sudīna-hṛdoya
bhaktivinoda, koriyā binoya,
śrī-ājñā-ṭahala koribe pracār

When will I feel compassion for all living beings? When will I forget my own pleasure in genuine humility? And when will I, Bhaktivinode, meekly go from door to door, preaching your message of love?

Ucchvāsa-nāma-kīrtana

THE ENLIVENING NAMES OF GAURA

(Bhaktivinode Thakur)

–1–

kali-kukkura-kadana jadi cāo he,
kaliyuga-pavana kali-bhaya-nāśana
śrī śacīnandana gāo he

If you want to subdue the dog of Kali, then sing out the names of Sri Sachi-nandan, who purifies the age of quarrel, putting an end to all fear.

–2–

gadādhara-mādana nitāyera prāṇa-dhana
advaitera prapūjita gorā
nimāñi viśvambhara śrīnivāsa īśvara
bhakta-samūha-cita-corā

He is Nimai, Visvambhara, the support of the universe, the intoxicator of Gadadhar Pandit, the life breath of Nitai, the worshipable object of Advaita Prabhu, the Lord of Srivasa Pandit, and the robber of the thoughts of all the other Nabadwip devotees.

–3–

nadīyā śaśadhara māyāpura-īśvara
nāma-pravartana-sura
gṛhi-jana-śikṣaka nyāsi-kula-nāyaka
mādhava rādhā-bhāva-pura

He is the moon over Nadia, the Lord of Mayapur; he is the divine being who has come to inaugurate the chanting of the Holy Names. He teaches the householders how to live and he leads the community of renunciates. He is Madhava, filled with the mood of Radha.

–4–

sārvabhauma-śodhana gajapati-tāraṇa
rāmānanda-poṣaṇa vīra
rūpānanda-vardhana sanātana-pālana
hari-dāsa-modana dhīra

He corrected Sarvabhauma Bhatt-acharya of his erroneous philosophical views; he delivered the King of Orissa, and he nourished Ramananda Raya's spiritual hunger like a hero. He increased the joy of Rupa Goswami, protected Sanatan Prabhu, and enlivened Hari Das Thakur like a sage.

–5–

vraja-rasa-bhāvana duṣṭa-mata-śātana
kapaṭi-vighātana-kāma
śuddha-bhakta-pālana śuṣka-jñāna-tāḍana
chala-bhakti-dūṣaṇa rāma

He was absorbed in thought of the moods of Vrindavan; he defeated the ideas of the wicked; he always desired to expose the hypocrites. He protected the pure devotees and showed the inadequacy of the god of the philosophers and the failures of pretentious devotion.

Śrī-Dāmodarāṣṭaka

EIGHT VERSES IN GLORIFICATION OF DAMODAR KRISHNA

(Śrī Satyavrata Muni)

–1–

namāmīśvaraṁ sac-cid-ānanda-rūpaṁ
lasat-kuṇḍalaṁ gokule bhrājamānam
yaśodā-bhiyolūkhalād dhāvamānaṁ
parāmṛṣṭam atyantato drutya gopyā

I offer my humble obeisances to the Supreme Lord, Sri Damodar, the supreme controller who possesses an eternal form of blissful knowledge, whose glistening earrings swing to and fro, who manifested himself in Gokula, who stole the butter that the gopis kept hanging from the rafters of their storerooms and who then quickly jumped up and ran in retreat in fear of Mother Yashoda but was ultimately caught.

–2–

rudantaṁ muhur netra-yugmaṁ mṛjantaṁ
karāmbhoja-yugmena sātaṅka-netram
muhuḥ śvāsa-kampa-trirekhāṅka-kaṇṭha-
sthita-graiva-dāmodaraṁ bhakti-baddham

Upon seeing his mother's whipping stick, he cried and rubbed his eyes again and again with His two lotus hands. His eyes were fearful and his breathing quick, and as Mother Yashoda bound His belly with ropes, he shivered in fright and his pearl necklace shook. To this Supreme

Lord, Sri Damodar, who is bound with his devotee's love, I offer my humble obeisances.

–3–

itīdṛk sva-līlābhir ānanda-kuṇḍe
sva-ghoṣaṁ nimajjantam ākhyāpayantam
tadīyeśita-jñeṣu bhaktair jitatvaṁ
punaḥ prematas taṁ śatāvṛtti vande

Those super excellent pastimes of Lord Krishna's babyhood drowned the inhabitants of Gokula in pools of ecstasy. To the devotees who are attracted only to his majestic aspect of Narayan in Vaikuntha, the Lord herein reveals: "I am conquered and overwhelmed by pure loving devotion." To the Supreme Lord, Damodar, my obeisances hundreds and hundreds of times.

–4–

varaṁ deva mokṣaṁ na mokṣāvadhiṁ vā
na cānyaṁ vṛṇe 'haṁ vareśād apīha
idaṁ te vapur nātha gopāla-bālaṁ
sadā me manasy āvirāstāṁ kim anyaiḥ

O Lord, although you are able to give all kinds of benedictions, I do not pray to you for liberation, nor eternal life in Vaikuntha, nor any other boon. My only prayer is that your childhood pastimes may constantly appear in my mind. O Lord, I do not even want to know your feature of Paramatma. I simply wish that your childhood pastimes may ever be enacted in my heart.

–5–

idaṁ te mukhāmbhojam atyanta-nīlair
vṛtaṁ kuṇḍalaiḥ snigdha-raktaiś ca gopyā
muhuś cumbitaṁ bimba-rakta-dharaṁ me
manasy āvirāstām alaṁ lakṣa-lābhaiḥ

O Lord, the cheeks of your blackish lotus face, which is encircled by locks of curling hair, have become reddened like bimba fruit due to Mother Yashoda's kisses. What more can I describe than this? Millions of opulences are of no use to me, but may this vision constantly remain in my mind.

–6–

namo deva dāmodarānanta viṣṇo
prasīda prabho duḥkha-jalābdhi-magnam
kṛpā-dṛṣṭi-vṛṣṭy-atidīnaṁ batānu
gṛhāṇeśa mām ajñam edhy akṣi-dṛśyaḥ

O unlimited Vishnu! O master! O Lord! Be pleased with me! I am drowning in an ocean of sorrow and am almost like a dead man. Please shower the rain of mercy on me; uplift me and protect me with your nectarean vision.

–7–

kuverātmajau baddha-mūrtyaiva yadvat
tvayā mocitau bhakti-bhājau kṛtau ca
tathā prema-bhaktiṁ svakāṁ me prayaccha
na mokṣe graho me 'sti dāmodareha

O Lord Damodara, in your form as a baby, Mother Yashoda bound you to a grinding stone with a rope for tying cows. You then freed the sons of Kuvera, Manigriva and Nalakuvera, who were cursed to stand as trees, and gave them the chance to become your devotees. Please bless me in this same way. I have no desire for liberation into your effulgence.

–8–

namas te 'stu dāmne sphurad-dīpti-dhāmne
tvadīyodarāyātha viśvasya dhāmne
namo rādhikāyai tvadīya-priyāyai
namo 'nanta-līlāya devāya tubhyam

O Lord, the entire universe was created by Lord Brahma, who was born from your abdomen, which was bound with a rope by Mother Yashoda. To this rope I offer my humble obeisances. I offer my obeisances to your most beloved Srimati Radharani and to your unlimited pastimes.

THE HARMONIUM-The harmonium is a western instrument that originated in Germany and England and became popular among immigrant pioneers in the American West in the nineteenth century. Around the same time, the British brought the harmonium to India, where it was quickly absorbed into the Indian music culture. Though not a traditional Indian instrument, it was admired for its portability and drone quality, which made it uniquely appropriate to the Indian aesthetic.

INSTRUMENTS

THE CELLO-The Cello was first made in its current shape in the mid 1600's. Its predecessor was the *viola da gamba* (Italian for knee fiddle), which had 6 or 7 strings and tied frets across its finger board. The current design of the cello allows the artist to play with a more melodic and expressive approach (instead of the *viola da gamba*'s chordal approach), a development consistent with the changes of European music during the seventeenth century.

MRIDANGA - The word mridanga is derived from *mrid* "clay" and *anga* "body," meaning that it is an instrument, a drum in this case, whose body or shell is made of clay. According to other sources, it derives from *mridan* and *ga*, meaning "beaten while moving," as its design permits the drum to be hung around the neck and played while walking or even dancing.

This instrument has a unique history connected to the cultural and spiritual revolution of Sri Chaitanya in sixteenth century Bengal. It is said that Sri Chaitanya ordered his associates to construct clay drums instead of the heavy and costly wooden drums.

A number of styles of mridanga playing developed known as Manoharshayi, Mandarini and Garanhati. These schools trace their lineages back to Srinivas Acharya, Shyamananda Pandit, and Narottam Das Thakur respectively. Though these ancient traditions have undergone change and are little practiced in their original form, the mridanga continues to be popular in Vaishnava sacred music.

According to the Manoharshayi school, Lord Krishna's flute pleaded with him not to be left behind when he incarnated as Sri Chaitanya. Krishna thus allowed the flute to accompany him in his advent as Sri Chaitanya in the mridanga form.

It is also said that Sri Chaitanya prayed to Lord Jagannath for the mantras with which to play the mridanga and the revelation of these mantras was given to Gadadhar Pandit who became the first player of this divine instrument.

Sri Mridanga pranam mantra:

namo jaganātha-sutāya
namo mṛdaṅga lavanāṅga-rasa-mādhurī
sahasra-guṇa-saṁyuktaṁ
namo mṛdaṅga namo namaḥ
namo baladevāya namo namaḥ

SARANGI-The sarangi is a bowed Indian fiddle with a goatskin top that is played with the cuticles of the left hand. It has three main strings and 36 resonating strings that are grouped into four different tuned sets. Unlike the sitar or sarod, which were played at the courts of medieval Indian nobility, the sarangi is considered to be a folklore instrument that was primarily used to accompany singers. Its popularity declined as the aforementioned instruments gained more and more recognition. The instrument used on this recording was built by Ricki Ram in Delhi and modified by Hans Christian.

NYCKELHARPA-The nyckelharpa is a bowed Scandinavian key fiddle, with four main strings and 12 resonating strings. The player pushes a set of wooden keys which in turn press against the strings. The nyckelharpa shares a common ancestry with another folk instrument, the hurdy gurdy, both of whose origins extend back to the Middle Ages.

SITARA -The sitara is a mini version of the Indian sitar with curved brass frets, four play strings, eight resonating strings, and two arched bridges that create the characteristic buzzing sound. The particular instrument played by Christian is custom made from solid ebony by a San Francisco Bay Area instrument maker.

Beevers, John. *The Autobiography of St. Therese of Lisieux: The Story of a Soul.* New York: Doubleday & Company, 1957.

Brown, Daniel P., Engler, Jack, and Wilber, Ken. *Transformations of Consciousness: Convention and Contemplative Perspectives on Development.* Boston: Shambala, 1986.

Das, Raghava Chaitanya. *Divine Name.* Chandigarh: HKT, 1998.

Maslow, Abraham H. *Religions, Values, and Peak-experiences.* New York: The Viking Press, 1974.

Puri, Swami B.P. *Art of Sadhana: a guide to daily devotion.* San Francisco: Mandala Publishing Group, 1999.

Sridhar, Bhakti Raksaka. *The Golden Volcano of Divine Love.* San Jose: Guardian of Devotion Press, 1984.

BIBLIOGRAPHY

Swami, A.C. Bhaktivedanta. *The Golden Avatar.* Philippines: Bhaktivedanta Book Trust, 1981.

Wilber, Ken. *Sex, Ecology, and Spirituality: The Spirit of Evolution.* Boston: Shambala, 1995.

Śrī-Prabhupāda-padma-stavaka — Hymn to Srila Prabhupada's lotus feet — 1
(Page 58)

Śaraṇāgati — Taking shelter — 2
(Page 62)

Śrī Gaura Nityānander Dayā — The mercy of Gaura-Nityananda — 3
(Page 63)

Dainyātmikā — A humble prayer — 4
(Page 64)

TRACK LIST

Śrī Śacīnandana Vandana — 5
(Page 65) — A hymn to the son of Sachi

Kabe Habe Bolo — 6
(Page 67) — When, O when, will that day be mine?

Ucchvāsa-nāma-kīrtana — 7
(Page 69) — The enlivening names of Gaura

Śrī-Dāmodarāṣṭaka — 8
(Page 70) — Eight verses in glorification of Damodar

SONG CREDITS

1. ***Śrī-Prabhupāda-padma-stavaka***

Agni Deva: lead vocals, kartals
Markandeya: mridanga
Vinode Vani: harmonium
Hans Christian: cello, bass, sarangi, bells, keyboards

2. ***Śaraṇāgati***

Agni Deva: lead vocals, kartals
Markandeya: mridanga
Vinode Vani: harmonium
Hans Christian: sitara, sarangi, fretless bass, keyboards
Kim Waters: shaker

3. ***Śrī Gaura Nityānandera Dayā***

Agni Deva: lead vocals, kartals
Markandeya: mridanga
Vinode Vani: harmonium
Hans Christian: cello, sitara, bass, keyboards

4. ***Dainyātmikā***

Agni Deva: lead vocals, kartals , small gong
Markandeya: mridanga
Vinode Vani: harmonium
Hans Christian: sarangi, cello, talking drum, frame drum, bells, keyboards

5. ***Śrī Śacīnandana Vandana***

Agni Deva: lead vocals, kartals, small gong
Markandeya: mridanga
Vinode Vani: harmonium
Hans Christian: nyckelharpa, cello, fretless bass, keyboards,
Kim Waters: shaker

6. ***Kabe Habe Bolo***

Agni Deva: lead vocals, kartals
Markandeya: mridanga, shaker
Vinode Vani: harmonium
Hans Christian: cello, sitara, tambura, bass, shaker beads
Kim Waters: shaker

7. ***Ucchvāsa-kīrtana***

Agni Deva: lead vocals, kartals
Markandeya: mridanga
Vinode Vani: harmonium
Hans Christian: sitara, fretless bass, keyboards
Bhima-Karma: additional kartals

8. ***Śrī-Dāmodarāṣṭaka***

Agni Deva: lead vocals, kartals
Markandeya: mridanga, shaker
Vinode Vani: harmonium
Hans Christian: sarangi, sitara, cello, nyckelharpa bass, keyboards, bells, handclaps
Kim Waters: shakers, handclaps

Chorus for all songs: Ramdas, Govardhan, Rati Keli, Bhima Karma, Krshangi, Kim Waters, Navadwip, Jaya Shri, Ananda Mayi and Sundar Gopal.

Produced by Hans Christian & Mandala Publishing

Recorded and mixed by Hans Christian at Allemande Productions, Fairfax, CA.

न्ममापि भगवन्ममापि नाम्नामकारि एतादृशी तव कृ

रागः तव भगवन्ममाऽऽनन्दाम्बुधिव दुर्दैवमीदृशमिहा

सहिष्णुना सहिष्णुना नाम्नामकारि तृणादपि सुनीचे

यि सदा हरिः सदा आनन्दाम्बुधिव अमानिना मानदे

गमये कीर्तनीय सदा हरिः स्तत्रार्पिता न धनं न जनं

मये सदा जन्मनीश्वरे आनन्दाम्बुधिव कवितां वा जग

विषमे भवाम्बुधौ सदा हरिः मम जन्मनि जन्म

विषमे भवाम्बुधौ भवताद्भक्तिरहैतुकी भवताद्भक्तिरहैतु

किङ्करं अयि नन्दतनुज! मम जन्मनि अयि नन्दतनुज!

धौ मां विषमे भवाम्बुधौ सदा हरिः पतितं मां विषमे

यि अयि विचिन्तय आनन्दाम्बुधिव कृपया तव पाद

य पादपङ्कज- अयि अयि नन्दतनुज! स्थितधूलीसदृशं